THIS BOOK
SHOULD ONLY BE USED
WITH ADULT SUPERVISION!

Written by Skye Wade
Illustrated by Arina Guryeva (Instagram: gnortsaverg)

ILLUSTRATED STEP-BY-STEP

Baking
Cookbook

• FOR KIDS •

VOL.
1

30 EASY AND DELICIOUS RECIPES

Hello, dear reader!

In this book, we use as few words as possible, so you can get right
down to baking. We don't like long, boring introductions either,
so go ahead and start creating culinary masterpieces.
You're sure to succeed because the recipes we've selected for you
are pretty simple but very tasty! Guaranteed!

Don't miss the important Safety Rules section — you want to cook
something delicious, not scrape dough off the ceiling.

We wish you culinary victories, young friend!

This book belongs to Chef

your name

CONTENTS

••• — difficulty

COOKING TIME

30 minutes

Easy Butter Cookies COOKIES AND BARS	32
Yogurt-Lemon Cookies COOKIES AND BARS	26
Russian Mini-Cake "Kartoshka" CUPCAKES & MUFFINS	138
Savoiardi Cookies COOKIES AND BARS	44
Quick Chocolate Croissant PASTRIES & BREADS	174
Easiest Oatmeal Cookies COOKIES AND BARS	20

40 minutes

Simple Pear Tarts PASTRIES & BREADS	180
Mini Deep Dish Pizzas (ready dough) SAVOURY AND SALTY	208
Lemon Poppy Seed Muffins CUPCAKES & MUFFINS	150

50 minutes

Molten Chocolate Cake CAKES	82
Banana Crumb Muffins CUPCAKES & MUFFINS	156
Crumbly Snowball Cookies COOKIES AND BARS	38
Chocolate-Nut Bars COOKIES AND BARS	50
Impossible Quiche SAVOURY AND SALTY	202

1 hour

Tarte Tatin CAKES	76
Fudgy Brownies with Pecans CAKES	104
Red Velvet Cupcakes CUPCAKES & MUFFINS	164
Fruit and Nut Bread PASTRIES & BREADS	186
Quick Apple Cake CAKES	118
Blueberry Muffins CUPCAKES & MUFFINS	144
Homemade Pizza (ready dough) SAVOURY AND SALTY	214

1.5 hours

Orange-Almond Cake CAKES	98
Strawberry Crumb Cake CAKES	90
Sponge Cake CAKES	70
Banana Bread PASTRIES & BREADS	192

4 hours

Tiramisu (ready Savoiardi cookies) CAKES	110

9 hours

Pistachio Macarons COOKIES AND BARS	58
Lemon Cheesecake CAKES	126

BEST FOR...

			Breakfast	Dinner
Cookies and Bars	Easiest Oatmeal Cookies	20	●	
	Yogurt-Lemon Cookies	26		
	Easy Butter Cookies	32		
	Crumbly Snowball Cookies	38		
	Savoiardi Cookies	44		
	Chocolate-Nut Bars	50	●	
	Pistachio Macarons	58		
Cakes	Sponge Cake	70	●	
	Tarte Tatin	76		
	Molten Chocolate Cake	82		
	Strawberry Crumb Cake	90		
	Orange-Almond Cake	98		
	Fudgy Brownies with Pecans	104		
	Tiramisu	110		
	Quick Apple Cake	118	●	
	Lemon Cheesecake	126		
Cupcakes & Muffins	Russian Mini-Cake "Kartoshka"	138		
	Blueberry Muffins	144	●	
	Lemon Poppy Seed Muffians	150	●	
	Banana Crumb Muffins	156	●	
	Red Velvet Cupcakes	164		
Pastries & Breads	Quick Chocolate Croissant	174	●	
	Simple Pear Tarts	180	●	
	Fruit and Nut Bread	186	●	
	Banana Bread	192	●	
Savory & Salty	Impossible Quiche	202	●	●
	Mini Deep Dish Pizzas	208	●	●
	Homemade Pizza	214		●

Picnic	Dessert	Birthday	Snack	Movie night	Christmas
●			●		
●			●		
	●		●		
●				●	
			●		
●			●	●	●
	●				●
	●				
	●	●			●
	●	●			●
●	●			●	●
	●			●	●
	●			●	●
	●	●			●
	●	●		●	●
	●	●			●
	●			●	
●				●	●
●				●	●
●			●	●	●
	●	●		●	●
●			●		
●			●		
●			●		
●			●	●	
●			●	●	
●			●	●	

1

Baking Basics

FOLLOW THE STEPS

1.

Read the Safety Rules!

2.

Wash your hands with soap and warm water.

3.

Clear enough space for working. Make it clean.

4.

Read your chosen recipe from start to end.

5.

Gather your ingredients, tools, and this book.

6.

Prepare your food. Warm the butter, wash fruits, etc.

7.

Carefully measure your ingredients.

8.

Check the position of the oven rack. It should be in the middle.

9.

Preheat the oven if needed.

10.

Follow the recipe to make the selected dish.

11.

Wash the dishes and utensils.

12.

Put everything back in its right place.

13.

Clean the kitchen up.

14.

Enjoy your food!

15.

Fill the notes page at the end of the recipe.

SAFETY RULES

General

 Make sure grown-ups are in the house and know what you are doing.

 When you see an "Adult Help" symbol, stop what you are doing and ask a grown-up to help you.

 Store food properly. Make sure it is fresh by checking at the expiry date and smelling it.

 Keep drawers and cabinet doors closed so you don't bump into or trip over them.

Electricity

 Keep all electrical equipment, cables, and plug away from water.

 Never touch switches with wet or damp hands.

Hygiene

 Wash your hands after touching raw eggs. Keep raw eggs away from foods you will not cook.

 After you have washed your hands, don't touch your phone, hair, face, etc.

 Cleaning supplies must be kept separately away from food.

 Clean up as you work. Throw away trash. Wipe up mess and spillage. Wet spots are slippery.

 Don't lick spoons, spatulas, etc. you are using for cooking. Don't taste raw butter and dough.

 Always use clean utensils to stop food spoiling quickly.

Appearance

Roll up long sleeves.
Tie back long hair or wear a hat.

Remove jewelry such as watches, rings, bracelets, etc.

Wear old clothes that are okay to dirty. Use an apron also.

Always wear shoes. They can help protect you from dropped knives, hot spills, and slippages.

Hot Things

Don't touch the stovetop or inside the oven with your hands.

Never leave cloths, empty dishes, or utensils on the stove.

Hold the pot handle while stirring to stop it from slipping off the stove.

Turn the pot handles to face away from you to avoid accidentally knocking them over.

Don't put glass or ceramic dishes on the stove or burner unless they are heatproof.

Use potholders for putting things into or taking things out of the oven. Ask grown-ups for help.

Never put plastic into the oven or on the stove. Never put metal into the microwave.

Don't place any hot dishes or saucepans directly onto the table or counter. Use hotpad.

Always use a timer, but don't leave the kitchen before everything is switched off.

Turn off the stove and oven when you have finished. Check it twice to be sure it is off.

Sharp Things

 Be careful with knife. Pick right size for your hand. It should be sharp. Curl your fingers under.

 Never leave knives on the edge of a table.

 Always use a cutting board when cutting or chopping things.

 Be careful when using graters, shredders, and peelers. Watch your fingers and take your time.

 Don't ever put your hands into a blender or food processor, even when food stuck in it.

 Always ask grown-ups to watch over you. Ask them to show how to chop, peel, grate and zest.

IF SOMETHING WENT WRONG,
first call for an adult!

 Pour baking soda onto small flames.

 If a fire is brewing in a pan, close it with a lid.

 If flames are large, leave the house and call 911.

Minor Burn

Place the burned area under running cool water. Apply an antiseptic spray or antibiotic ointment and wrap a gauze bandage.

Minor Cuts and Scrapes

Wash your hands. Stop the bleeding with a gauze pad. Apply petroleum jelly. Cover the cut with a sterile bandage.

BAKING LANGUAGE

Batter

a liquid, flour-based mixture

Beat

to make the butter fluffy

Chop

to cut into small pieces

Double Boil

to melt over a pot of boiling water

Dough

a thick, flour-based mixture

Dust

to sprinkle a thin layer

Fold

to gently mix in something light

Garnish

to decorate

Glaze

to coat with a shiny layer

Grate

to shred with a grater

Grease

to coat a baking dish with butter or oil

Knead

to squash dough with your hands

Line

to cover with parchment paper

Melt

to heat something solid until it's liquid

Peel

to remove the rind with a peeler

Pipe

to squeeze from the piping bag

Preheat

to heat an oven in advance

Punch

to push down to squeeze out a gas

Rise

to let the dough get bigger

Simmer

to heat without bringing to a boil

Sift

to process through a sieve

Stir

to mix slowly

Whip

make egg whites or cream foamy

Whisk

to mix with a whisk until uniform

Zest

to remove the surface layer of citrus

HOW TO MEASURE

Liquid. Large amount.

Use a measuring cup. Pour in the liquid until it reaches the right level on the side of the cup.

Liquid. Small amount.

Pour the liquid carefully into a measuring spoon. Do it over a bowl to catch any spills.

Dry ingredients

Pour the ingredient into the measuring cup or spoon. Use a butter knife to make it flat.

Butter

Use measurement marks on the package. Cut down through the wrapper at the correct mark.

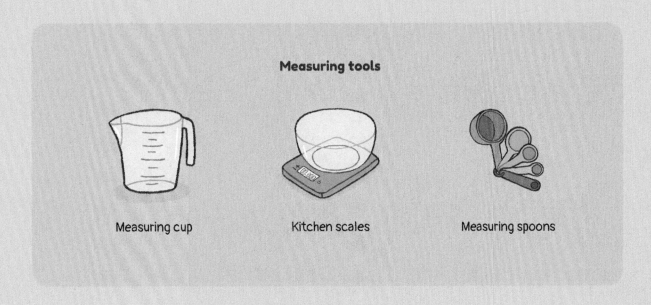

Measuring tools

Measuring cup   Kitchen scales   Measuring spoons

2

Cookies and Bars

Easiest Oatmeal Cookies

3 INGREDIENTS   DIFFICULTY:

This amazing and healthy cookie recipe can make an oatmeal lover out of anyone.

Let these cookies literally "float your boat" with their unforgettable flavors, great for any cookie jar, bake sale, treat tray, or dessert day, your way!

10 min

20 min

3 cookies

PREP TIME   BAKING   YIELD